little chickin's name

given by

PIGGLES' CHOICE

A FARM GRUB Feed Tale

written by Katherine Moore
illustrated by Mark Braught
wrangled by Mother Hen

PIGGLES' CHOICE, A FARM GRUB Feed Tale

Text by Katherine Moore

Illustrations © Mark Braught

Art Direction by Don Grant

Wrangled by Mother Hen

Special Nutrition Tips by Emily C. Harrison MS, RD, LD.
Curriculum Research by Maya Jenkins, Dean of Curriculum & Assessment, ANCS.

Editorial Assistance from Lucy & Will Chickin.

© 2011 Chickin Feed, LLC
Published by the Chickin Feed Press. All rights reserved.
www.chickinfeed.com

ISBN-13 97800-9819181-2-9
ISBN-10 0-9819181-2-3
Library of Congress Control Number: 2011915416

To all the little chickins,

**May you choose well in
all that you pursue.**

– Mother Hen

To parents and caregivers,

We are the single most important
"health educators" in our children's lives.
Live by example, make good choices and have fun
with your chickins.

– Leslie Smith Grant
(Mother Hen)

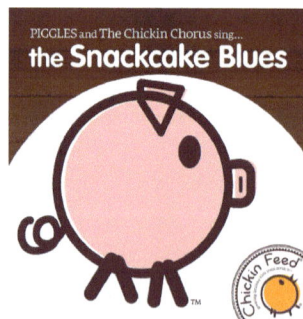

PIGGLES and The Chickin Chorus sing....

the Snackcake Blues

™

Chickin Feed

Hear PIGGLES sing her hit song

"Snackcake Blues"

(see back of book for details)

PIGGLES likes to sing.
She chooses the blues.

PIGGLES likes to dance.
She mostly moonwalks
in the mud.

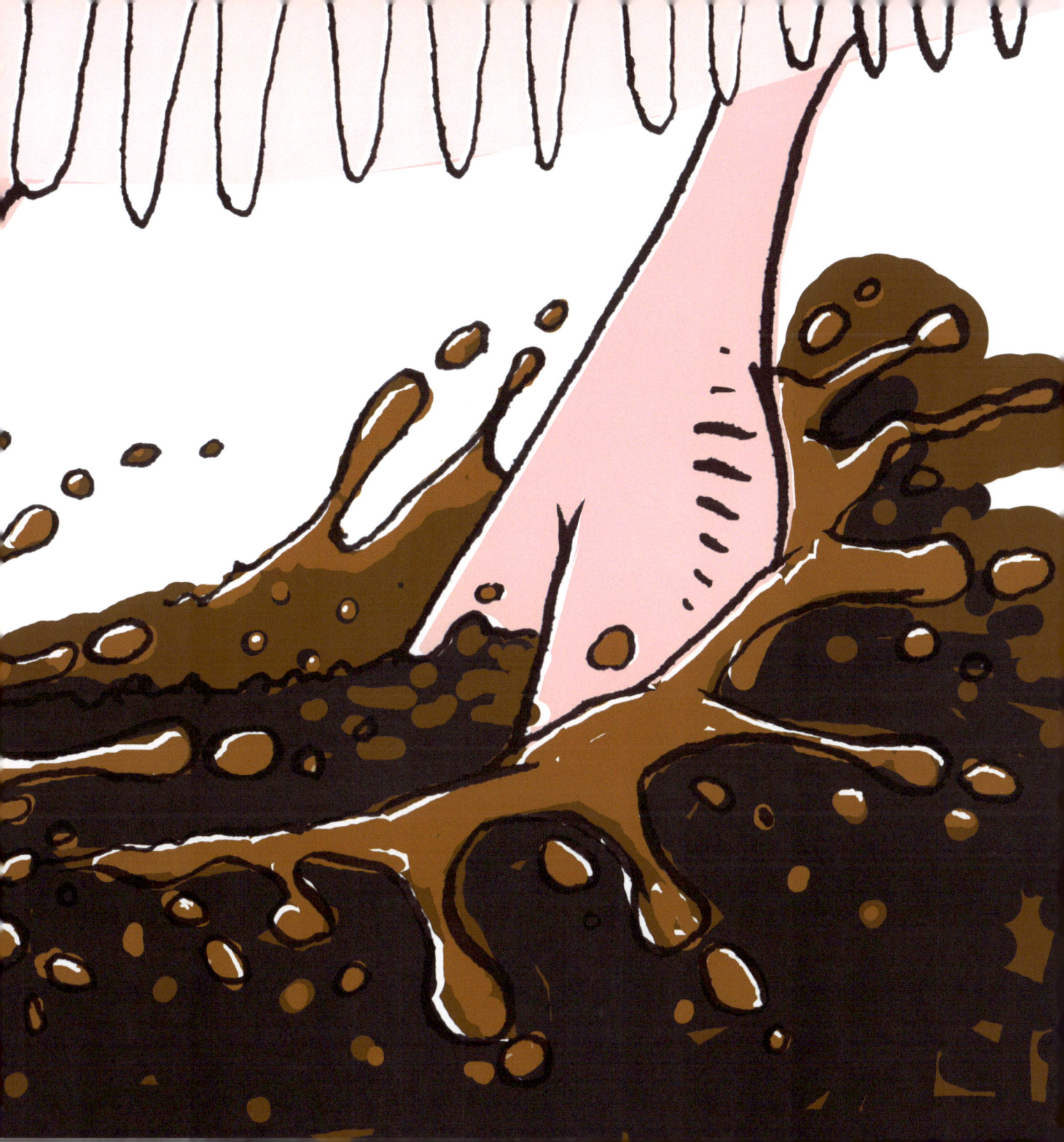

PIGGLES likes to play with her friends.
She prefers to play
Pirates and
Princesses.

But most of all, PIGGLES **loves** to eat!

But WAIT, PIGGLES! WAIT!

REAL FOOD, growing food

makes you strong.

Treats go last...

where they belong.

FARMER GOAT says,
"If you choose ONLY treats like that . . .

Chances are you'll sing real flat!"

"But if REAL FOOD
is what you choose to eat".

And DUCKIE declares,
"If you choose only treats
for your meals . . .

But,
if "growing foods" are
on your plate.

Just wait!
Your dance moves
will be great.

PIGGLES CHOOSES REAL FOOD!
Yay!

Now she can play with her friends all day.

REAL FOOD, Growing Food, makes you strong...

TREATS go last, where they belong.

The End.
(almost)

"Special Tips from the Nutrition Chick"

by Emily C. Harrison, MS, RD, LD.

www.dancernutrition.com

Parents have the power to help kids make great choices by ensuring that they have easy access to 3-4 servings of veggies and 2-3 servings of fruit everyday.

Keep fruit and ready-to-eat veggies at eye level so kids can easily spot them and make smart choices all by themselves. Feeling independent is key with young children.

Prepare little containers of convenient healthy snacks in a hurry. Bite-sized fruits and veggies like apples, oranges, bananas, dried cranberries, raisins, berries, carrots, cucumbers, peppers, tomatoes, etc. can be packaged in small, kid-friendly containers. It will take a little bit of planning, but it will pay off in a big way when your "convenience food" is actually healthy!

Grab-and-go healthy snacks, that your children know are special for them, will win out over junk foods – but only if it is convenient.

Limit access to soft drinks or sugary juices. They aren't the best way to hydrate – DRINK WATER! Also, the empty calories may fill your child up and prevent them from wanting to eat their "growing foods." Remember that sugary drinks are TREATS and for special times only!

Just as PIGGLES must make choices when presented with delicious looking treats, our children must learn at a very early age to choose well – as parents and caregivers, we can choose to stack the deck in favor of healthy choices by providing easy access to healthy foods.

*For more of Emily's "highly digestible" NUTRITION INFO…see the Nutrition chapter in
The Chickin Feed Primer | a useful companion for modern families
available in the Feed Store at www.chickinfeed.com.

"Not so ho-hum" Curriculum

fun ways to teach little chickins about
making healthy choices

written by Mother Hen

with research assistance by Maya Jenkins,
Dean of Curriculum & Assessment, ANCS

HOST A PIGGLES PARTY

READ   PIGGLES CHOICE to your class.

DISCUSS

- Which foods do they recognize in the book?

- Which foods have they tried?

- Which food groups are each of the foods in? Talk about the different food groups.

    - Grain / Bread / Pasta (WHOLE grains are awesome!)
        Great for long lasting energy, essential vitamins and fiber.
    - Veggies & Fruits
        These two groups should make up about half of our diet each day. They help
        our brains to work well, our eyes to see, our boo boos to heal, and
        provide important vitamins and minerals for long healthy lives. It is
        important to eat a wide variety - lots of colors from the rainbow!
    - Protein (Fish / Meat / Beans)
        Important for muscle building, repair and making healthy blood! (Cue
        Count Dracula)
    - Calcium/Dairy
        Growing strong healthy bones is a great thing! Dairy is a great way to get
        calcium.
    - Sweets/Extras
        Very important to limit the amount of sweets and and treats so our bellies
        have room for our GROWING FOODS. If a small treat comes after our grow-
        ing food, it won't give us the "snackcake blues."

- What did PIGGLES want to eat?

- What did FARMER GOAT tell her? **(REAL FOOD, growing food makes you strong...
  treats go last where they belong)**

- What did PIGGLES end up choosing?

- Ask WHY we eat food in the first place? **Food is the fuel for our bodies – it makes us able
  to think and grow well. It helps us run like fuel makes our cars run.**

cont.

PIGGLES PARTY notes...
and don't for get the tunes!

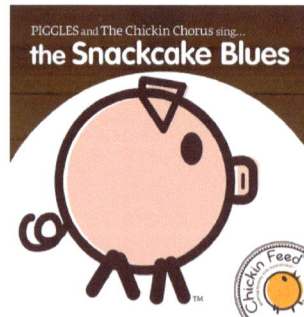

PIGGLES and The Chickin Chorus sing...
the Snackcake Blues

Chickin Feed

preview at www.chickinfeed.com/farm-grub/piggles/
AND
download it at www.cdbaby.com

HOST A PIGGLES PARTY cont.

INVITE: Invite parents, or other classes to your PIGGLES Party. Children can draw pictures of their favorite fruits and veggies, and use the drawings for invitations. Have them count how many total invitations there are. Did anyone choose the same foods? How many chose each food?

FIELD TRIP: Arrange a field trip to a local Farmers' Market, Dairy, Community Garden or Farm (please don't visit a pig farm on this field trip - PIGGLES might be upset with some of the questions.) Purchase something during your visit or ask the gardener if you may harvest something to bring back to class. It is important to tie the "non-grocery store" experience to a food source and bringing back something you will prepare for your PIGGLES Party.

PREPARE: Ask each child bring in one of their favorite fruits or veggies from home to supplement what you purchased on your field trip if necessary. Add some hummus and pita to round out the menu if you are trying to replace a meal. Serve WATER to drink - sqeeze in some fresh lime. Where possible, have them help clean and cut the produce. ONLY after they wash their hands. Talk about how important it is to have clean hands when they work with food.

Talk about the fact that you are celebrating your PIGGLES Party by making good choices to eat REAL FOOD instead of snackcakes and sweet treats.

PARTY: Let the children talk as much as they can about the foods they serve. Where they came from, who grew them and how they prepared them. Put on your PIGGLES and The Chickin Chorus tune "Snackcake Blue" and see if they can pantomime their way through the song.

Enjoy your PIGGLES Party!
– one party that won't end in "sugar shock."

The End.
(for real)

www.ingramcontent.com/pod-product-compliance
Lightning Source LLC
Chambersburg PA
CBHW041547040426
42447CB00002B/77